PRINCEWILL LAGANG

16 GOLDEN RULES TO A SUCCESSFUL MARRIAGE FOR WOMEN

First published by Lagang Princewill 2024

Copyright © 2024 by Princewill Lagang

This novel is entirely a work of fiction. The names, characters and incidents portrayed in it are the work of the author's imagination. Any resemblance to actual persons, living or dead, events or localities is entirely coincidental.

Princewill Lagang asserts the moral right to be identified as the author of this work.

First edition

This book was professionally typeset on Reedsy.
Find out more at reedsy.com

Contents

1   Introduction   1

2   Play and Have Fun Together   3

3   Bathroom Decorum   5

4   Massage and Romance   7

5   Love Affirmations   9

6   The Act of Romantic Text Message and Phone Calls   11

7   A Warm Welcome   13

8   Buy a Gift   15

9   A Special Day for a Special Award   17

10   Celebrate his Birthday Elaborately   19

11   Avoid Disrespect from Anyone   21

12   Appreciation Time   23

13   Be at your best at the Kitchen   25

14   Good Dressing, Good Attractions   27

15   Marital Support   29

16   Bedroom Matters   31

17   Consistent Love and Appreciation   33

One

Introduction

The woman/wife plays a major role in a family, she makes and keeps the home, you cannot underestimate the power of a woman as to making and keeping a home, in terms of house chores, feeding, and taking good care of her children and husband. While the Man goes out there to work, a woman is saddled majorly to take care of the home.

In this book, you will find the opportunity to know and interface with our 16 golden rules to a successful marriage for women, women need to know these 16 golden rules in order to avoid divorce and broken homes. We all agree that a man has needs and his needs are enormous, from the dinning table to the bedroom, there is no doubt that those women who know how to keep a man will also know how to keep their marriages and family. Women need to know that they have the power to access the heart of any man and this power is not with their mouth but with the kind acts and demonstration

1

of love through body languages and emotional affections.

Two

Play and Have Fun Together

A s a woman you should engage in playing with your husband or spouse. Sometimes a little smile and laughter goes a long way to spice things up in your marriage, although there are times when you'll need to be serious and point out certain issues about the family to him but don't be too serious at all times. Put romance and playfulness in your daily schedule, examine his mood, mostly after eating, when he is satisfied and feeling great, when you go out for shopping or site seeing to parks and recreational centres, these are moments you must not let slide, a little joke here and there, a little spank on the buttocks, a little hide and seek play will go a long way to brighten his day.

Remember, men are always on the receiving aspect when it comes to job and work duties, greater task are always given to the men, the average man does not get any kind of pampering or favour at the market place, stress is part of his lifestyle by default. He goes to work and receives a lot of back lashes from his boss to his clients and all he wants is to make his family proud by providing all the necessary things needed at home. A proud man will never want his wife to take on his responsibility at home and he always look forward to coming back home to meet a cozy and warm welcome from his loving and caring wife. Look for ways to laugh together. Say something funny and do something funny. Play and have fun together. Do not allow another woman do for your husband what you should be doing to keep your home together.

Three

Bathroom Decorum

⦿⦿⦿

I nvite your husband to a bath at night, especially at night. Bathing alone can be boring at times, so instead of allowing him do that alone, you can employ the practice of bathing together, it eases the stress, especially when a little massage here and there is involved, a romantic bath and send relaxation signals to his brain, making him feel loved and appreciated by his loving and darling wife. A lot of women, especially African women, don't know the effect of these practices until they try it secretly.

The reason why your husband prefers to stay for long at the bear parlour or at the soccer viewing centre is because he does not want to come to a home where a nagging wife is waiting to nag, correct his errors or flaws, look down on him or compare him with other men in her life, maybe her father, her pastor or her ex husband or boyfriend.

Enjoy the pleasure of bathing together. Showering with your spouse is sweet, intimate, and a great way to get fully comfortable with each other's bodies.

Tell him to help you scrub your back as you bathe together. Play together in the bathroom and if it leads to sex, then you have your husbands full attention, remember say sweet words of affirmations and play with him while taking your bath together, words are powerful agents to soften the heart of a man.

Four

Massage and Romance

There should be special moments within the week when you give your husband a serious massage, the pleasure he should have gotten from a female masseuse can be gotten at home and in your bedroom, the act of massaging your husband will affirm that you love and care for him, it also affirms that you are aware of the stress he is going through at his work place.

Giving your husband a shoulder, back, and neck massage in the bathroom, bedroom, and living room as often as possible will go a long way to spice things up in your marriage. It will register a long time memory, he will long for another time for a good massage by his loving and caring wife.

You don't need to be an expert to give your spouse a good message. Ask your spouse to lie on his body, take your time to touch some sensitive aspects of his body and observe his reactions, he will definitely tell you to concentrate on some soft spots because he is feeling the romance from your hands. It is also good that both of you visit a masseuse, but its better when both of your massage each other to promote the bonding between you and your spouse.

Five

Love Affirmations

Say "I love you"

In this chapter we will examine the act of love in words, the reason why verbal affirmations are a sign of a heart that truly loves, and how it plays a major role in keeping marriages afloat and lively. Now it's a norm that men are the ones that always have to use the phrase 'I Love You' in relationships being that women are emotional beings and one of their love languages is in words, but today we will turn the table around.

Surprisingly men also love to hear sweet words of affirmation from their wives or spouse, not just to narrow it to 'I Love You' but other sweet words of affirmations like; 'thank you', 'you are the best thing that happened to me', 'you are so sweet my darling husband', 'I am sincerely sorry', 'My Sincere Apology', 'You can do it', 'I believe in you my darling husband', 'We can pull through together', 'I will support you',.

Tell him and show him you love him so much. Tell him how he's the greatest man on earth, tell him how that he's your best man, tell him how that his voice awakens your soul, always use a pet name to acknowledge his presence or attend to his needs. It is not only women that are moved by what they hear. Men are moved by what they hear too. Remember, if your man does not get these affirmations from you as his wife or spouse, its possible, he will hear it either from the restaurant, or his office or his place of business and that's not a competition you want to get into. So mount your guards, take hold of your man and be in charge of your family.

Six

The Act of Romantic Text Message and Phone Calls

This is also a love language to men generally, why is it that in some cases, a woman is already asleep but a man can be on phone, replying messages and voice notes from numerous ladies who see him as a great person and they wish he was theirs, its not really true that he's their best but it gets to the man when love messages are sent to him privately, so women must learn to keep their husbands or spouse through romantic phone calls, chats or text messages.

You can also go the extra mile to send your romantic pictures to remind him of what a beauty he has back at home, make sure they arouse his feelings so that he can hurry back home to meet you. Call him and tell him that you miss him and you can't wait for him to be back home, call him and tell him that you prepared his favourite meal, let him know how much you want him in the bedroom, call him and tell him you have a surprise for him once he's back early.

Call, email, or send a romantic text message to him when you're apart so he knows you are thinking of him. Call him on phone whenever he goes out just to say, "I love you", and you can't wait to see him back home. Remember, if your husband does not get back early from work, something or someone is definitely taking his attention, so you must step up your game in other to be his first on the list of his priorities.

Seven

A Warm Welcome

⚬⚭⚬

A home without a man will affect a lot of things, it will affect the growth of the kids, it will affect stability in provisions, it will affect the woman emotionally and almost ruin the relationship between the man and his wife so when your husband comes back from the office, meet him as if this is what you have been waiting for all day. Smile at him. Give him a kiss and a hug. Don't have a sour face. Smile when you see him always and welcome him home with a hug. Let him know you are happy to see him. Help him unbutton his shirt as he undresses after an outing.

Make sure he gets a warm bath, and after which there's is dinner served already, serve him yourself, look into his eyes and ask him how the food taste. Men are visionary beings, they are mostly moved by what they see, so its absolutely necessary to welcome your husband back home with a warm smile, put on what makes you look inviting and touch him where he can feel your vibrations. Give him a peck on the cheek and whisper into his ears; 'you are welcome home my king', leak his ears and smile at him.

These romantic acts go a long way to telling your husband that you still cherish him and love him sincerely, he now believes that he's the best thing that happened to you. He will stop feeling you are still stuck to your ex and he now has your attention, with these acts he won't think of another woman, the mistake most women make is to believe that their husbands have no other woman in their lives besides them. That's not so true, every man has the potential of attracting another woman, especially when they are successful and hardworking, the same attributes and peculiarities you saw in your husband that made you fall in love with him, are same attributes other women also see. So with this, what makes you think that they won't be attracted to him?

Eight

Buy a Gift

When was the last time you bought a gift for your husband? When was the last time you surprised him with a gift of some kind that he'd enjoy having this month. Buy him a new set of underwear. Buy him new pair of socks, belts, shoes, shirts, trousers, wristwatch or phone. Nothing is too small or big to give to your dear husband.

At this point, we can tell if you really know your husband by the gift you get for him, and sincerely you don't have to buy a car or a house, the little things matter a lot, men appreciate the little gifts that make them proud to say; 'My wife bought this for me', it makes other men jealous.

Most at times, men are on the receiving side in the society, they almost do not get any treats of favour of any sought when they are out there working hard to make ends meet for their family. But the truth is, deep down, they long for a treat, they long for an appreciation, they long to be helped and assisted, so as a wife, when you make it a duty to surprise your husband with gifts, he always will cherish you, and trust me, with this show of love, he will almost meet your needs anytime you have a need.

Nine

A Special Day for a Special Award

Give your husband these types of awards "Husband of the Year Award", "Father of the Year Award" or "Lover of the Year Award". Organize a special ceremony to celebrate this, it could be on his birthday, it could be at a festive season, it could be at your own birthday, it could be at a vacation, it could be at a wedding anniversary, it could be on a world fathers day or mothers day.

Dedicate any award you receive or any book you write to your spouse. It shows you are proud of him to flaunt him as your source of inspiration, your personal assistant in your research work or academic pursuit.

Awards are affirmations that you hold your husband in high esteem, you see him as your head, even when it seem you are smarter or more intelligent, when you present your husband an award, it shows you put him ahead of you, it makes him proud of the kind of woman he married, it makes him see you as a submissive wife and one who acknowledges his role in your life as your lead man.

Ten

Celebrate his Birthday Elaborately

~~~~~~

Make sure to have your husband's birth date handy, don't ever wake up one day and say; 'Oh I forgot its your birthday' Don't take his birthday for granted. Pray, Plan and Prepare for his special day. Remember, that was the day he was born, without which you won't be with him, celebration is also a way to tell God thank you for creating my husband and giving him to me as a gift.

Call his friends, your friends, and your families to remind them of his birthday. Tell them to call and pray for him. Make a post on facebook or any other social media handles and tag your husband, make sure the post is touching and creative to express how much you love and respect him as your husband.

Always make every year's celebration different from the other previous year, always make sure to keep surprising him and increasing the level of celebration on a yearly basis. Start planning at least 3 months before the birthday month for your husband's birthday.

Take him out to a place he longed to be and give him that treat he deserves back at home, make sure your bedroom is inviting on that faithful day, make sure to serve him breakfast in bed. Make sure to decorate the house in honour of his celebration, let the kids and anyone who visits the house that day know that there is a special celebration of life going on that very day.

Use his birthday to renew your marital vows to each other, and personally pray for your husband that day, don't be carried away by the celebration without praying or giving him great wishes that will encourage him and motivate him to keep dreaming and pursuing his dreams and ambition.

Eleven

Avoid Disrespect from Anyone

Men see true love as honour and respect, above all these acts of love and affirmations, respect is everything to a man. Men are proud beings, there's a king in every man, there is a Lord in every man, there is a quest to be known and seen as a great person in every man.

Let the respect start from you and from your children, never allow family members or friends to treat him disrespectfully: Defend him before anyone who dishonors him or trivializes his position as your husband. This is a love language that can never be under estimated. It affirms that you cherish and honour your husband, it affirms that you put him ahead of yourself. It makes him proud to be your husband.

Even when you are not there to defend him, he will long to come back home so that he can get that love, affection, and attention he needs from his beloved wife. Make moves to resolve any issues he has with anyone, whether they are friends, family or business partners, but always do it in his favour.

Don't just resolve issues on his behalf but give him advice that will avoid unnecessary disrespect or dishonour from anyone out there or even from your children. Always look out for him at all times, when he sees that you have his business or job at heart, he will love you more, because a man's heart is usually where his money is and he gradually will place you above his money in the order of priority.

Twelve

Appreciation Time

~~~~~~~~~~

Appreciate his efforts, just a word like; 'thank you', 'I Love and appreciate you', even when he's performing and when he's not able to perform, men like to be appreciated at all times. Nothing provokes a man to perform than appreciation, when he is appreciated, he goes the extra mile to see that he lives up to expectations as regarding his fatherly duties in the family.

A man that is truly and sincerely appreciated will go all out for his wife and family, he now knows that you value his efforts in the house, even when the wife earns more income than him, he will always reciprocate the kind gesture at the slightest means possible. He will also learn to say; 'thank you'.

Appreciation can also be in action and not only in words, your response as a wife to his personal needs in the bedroom will often tell how much you appreciate his efforts, a little massage here and there, a little romance here and there and making love to him will almost reveal the intent of your heart towards your husband.

Thirteen

Be at your best at the Kitchen

⚜

In the aspect of cooking, no matter intelligent and creative you are as a wife, you cannot have it all, always be ready to learn, unlearn and relearn, go for trainings and invite someone who is specialised in certain dishes to teach and train you privately and cook his food promptly.

Specially serve him. Treat him like a king. Serve your husband as your king. Special plates are for your husband, not for your pastor or visitors. Don't just cook his food alone, serve it specially. Learn to cook new dishes, also learn to improve on what you already know, change your recipe from once and again. Don't delegate serving your husband to someone else.

Some women have lost their husbands because they ignored his stomach, it is often said, that the way to a man's heart is his stomach, even if you are a career woman and you employ a cook, make sure it's a male cook, and if it's a female cook, make sure you can trust the lady. Be the one to serve your husband yourself, wear something sexy when cooking and serving your husband. Treat him like a VIP. Treat him like a special guest on the dining table.

While eating on the dinning table, engage the method of feeding each other to spice up your dinning experience.

Fourteen

Good Dressing, Good Attractions

I t has been said; 'dress to be addressed'. Most often a lot of people get carried away by their dressing at home, they always feel you're only to be cautious of your dressing when you're out for a meeting, event or work. In this chapter we advice wives, dress to attract your husband always.

Every man loves a good-looking and attractive woman, be that woman for your husband. Don't stop looking good because you are now married, don't allow another woman use her jezebelic act of dressing to seduce your husband, be the one that always put him on fire whenever he sees you.

Walk like a beauty queen, your walking and standing posture also matters, don't walk anyhow, don't get familiar with your husband and dress unintentionally. Put on a smiling face, it has been proven that it takes more muscles to frown than to smile, and those who laugh a lot live longer.

Properly compose yourself, don't do things anyhow in the house, take your time and walk and look good in your home Get attractive cloths (gowns and underwears) for private use. Wear what he loves to see, Invest in sexy attires that turn him on when you are with him. Let him long to have you always, avoid dressing like an old woman, you will succeed in driving your husband far from you even when he still lives in same building with you.

Fifteen

Marital Support

~⁂~

Nothing heals a broken heart like emotional and intentional acts of support, support can come in several ways, like; supporting his vision, goals, dreams and ambitions, reminding him how great of a man he is. Buy books that pertain to his career and vision.

PRAY FOR YOUR HUSBAND ALWAYS, supporting your husband spiritually is not out of place, encouraging him that God has not forgotten him goes a long way to boost his faith in God. Most at times, women often make the mistake to think that it's solely the duty of the husband to carry the spiritual burden of the home, but some wives have proven that to not so correct. We now have women who pray and seek God on behalf of their husbands and family and God will always answer a woman's prayer faster than a man's prayer, biblical examples have proven it to be so.

Believe in your husband. Make him know that you believe in him and his vision. Be his number-one fan. Show him how much you believe in him by making enquires and planning to get breakthroughs in his career or business, even seeking for a better job for your husband is not out of place. Do this and thank me later.

Sixteen

Bedroom Matters

ake your bedroom a sex sanctuary, when the bedroom is sexually inviting, be intentional about the choice of colours for the interior, keep it clean, neat, and smelling fresh at all times, don't use your bedroom as a place to throw your dirty laundry or trash. Worship your bed and make it cozy enough for relaxation.

Remember, as the wife you are the lead in the bedroom, on the bed you decide what becomes of your home and husband. On your bed, you have the power to influence any decisions your husband will make in life. Understand the art of sex properly and know your husbands best sex positions, be a goddess in your bedroom.

Often times, women don't like to ask questions regarding sex and love making as this is a very sensitive topic, but the truth is no one has it all when it comes to this topic, no matter what you know before now, there is always something to learn when it comes to sex and love making, this is so because men are differently wire in certain ways, and what is good for this man may not be good for the other man, so the learning never stops.

It's not how long the sex or can be that matters, its what satisfies your husband that matters, so engaging in fore plays can be a very important way to engage a sexual urge from your husband. Make it a special time and not a daily routine, let him long for you and see it as a privilege whenever you both are at it, be in charge as well, don't always allow him to do the whole work on bed.

Seventeen

Consistent Love and Appreciation

Y ou have come this far not to stop or be inconsistent, continue to show love to your husband, in so many ways, try your best to reveal another aspect of love and appreciation even if you don't receive it.

According to the law of harvest; 'you reap what you sow'. Keep doing what is needed, even when its not reciprocated, every man long to be treated nicely, they want a consistent and long lasting love affair.

Spice up your marriage with the above mentioned acts of love and see your marriage thrive.

Milton Keynes UK
Ingram Content Group UK Ltd.
UKHW021014291124
451807UK00015B/1249